To: Toni

From: The

Baldens

Every Woman Should Have a Blowtorch

Fiery Thoughts for Feisty Females

Written and compiled by
the Editors of Peter Pauper Press

Illustrations by Kerrie Hess

 PETER PAUPER PRESS, INC.
White Plains, New York

Designed by Heather Zschock

Copyright © 2010
Peter Pauper Press, Inc.
202 Mamaroneck Avenue
White Plains, NY 10601
All rights reserved
ISBN 978-1-4413-0329-5
Printed in China
7 6 5 4 3 2 1

Visit us at www.peterpauper.com

Every Woman Should Have a Blowtorch

Fiery Thoughts for Feisty Females

Contents

Introduction

"**E**very woman should have a blowtorch," Julia Child once said as she commenced to caramelize the top of a *crème brûlée*. And every woman could use a dish of empowering *bons mots* every so often as well. *Voilà!* Here you are—the perfect little book of wit and wise-cracks from some of our sassier sisters (and a few outrageous dudes). Stand back as these outspoken free spirits shine their piercing light on men, love, marriage, life, work, and more, inspiring you to join the ranks of fiercesome females past and present, while holding this truth to be self-evident: "You only live once, but if you do it right, once is enough."

chapter 1

Us & Them

(Women & Men)

My idea of
superwoman is
someone who
scrubs her
own floors.

Bette Midler

Of all the wild
beasts of land
or sea, the wildest
is woman.

Menander

A woman is
like a tea bag.
You never know
how strong she
is until she gets
into hot water.

Eleanor Roosevelt

There is nothing
like the sound of women
really laughing. The roaring
laughter of women is like the
roaring of the eternal sea.

Mary Daly

Women have got
to make the world
safe for men since
men have made it
so darned unsafe
for women.

Lady Nancy Astor

It's called
civilization.
Women invented
it, and every time
you men blow it
all to bits, we just
invent it again.

Tina, **The Folk of the Fringe**
by Orson Scott Card

What I don't understand is how women can pour hot wax on their bodies, let it dry, then rip out every single hair by its root and still be scared of spiders.

Jerry Seinfeld

The bikini is the most important invention since the atom bomb.

Diana Vreeland

What would men be without women? Scarce, sir, mighty scarce.

Mark Twain

The curve is
more powerful
than the sword.

Mae West

chapter 2

Love
&
Marriage

Love is like playing checkers. You have to know which man to move.

Jackie "Moms" Mabley

19

I'm not good at being alone. Especially at the end of the day when my finances are a mess, my car is falling apart, [and] I can't find my shoes. That's when I need a big strong guy to hold me close so I can look deep into his eyes and blame him.

Simone Alexander

Bigamy is having one husband too many. Monogamy is the same.

Anonymous
confirmed bachelorette

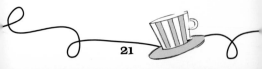

I love being married.
It's so great to find that
one special person you
want to annoy for the
rest of your life.

Rita Rudner

Behind every successful man is a surprised woman.

Maryon Pearson

My husband
said he needed
more space. So I
locked him outside.

Roseanne Barr

chapter 3

Bad Grrrls

I don't have the time every day to put on makeup. I need that time to clean my rifle.

Henriette Mantel

Revenge is sweet.
Sweeter than
tiramisu.

Kathy Lette

When I'm good, I'm very good, but when I'm bad, I'm better.

Mae West

Enemies are so stimulating.

Katharine Hepburn

There are
thousands of Sioux
in this valley. I am
not afraid of them.
They think I am a
crazy woman and
never molest me . . .
I guess I am the only
human being they
are afraid of.

Calamity Jane

I have often wished I had time to cultivate modesty, but I am too busy thinking about myself.

Dame Edith Sitwell

chapter 4

Work

Women's place is in the House— and the Senate.

Gloria Schaffer

I'm extraordinarily patient, provided I get my own way in the end.

Margaret Thatcher

I don't seem able
to do my best
unless I'm behind
or in trouble.

Babe Didrikson Zaharias

Besides Shakespeare and me, who do you think there is?

Gertrude Stein

If an opportunity scares you, that's God's way of saying you should jump at it.

Anna Quindlen

Though the sex
to which I belong
is considered weak
you will nevertheless find
me a rock that bends
to no wind.

Queen Elizabeth I

39

With a pencil
and paper,
I could revise
the world.

Alison Lurie

Don't live down
to expectations. Go out
there and do something
remarkable.

Wendy Wasserstein

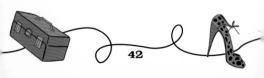

I don't mind how much my ministers talk—as long as they do what I say.

Margaret Thatcher

chapter 5

Faith
&
Family

I know God won't give me anything I can't handle. I just wish He didn't trust me so much.

Mother Teresa

I am not afraid . . . I was born to do this.

Joan of Arc

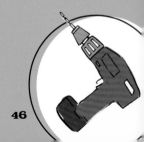

46

[That little man in black says] woman can't have as much rights as man because Christ wasn't a woman. Where did your Christ come from? . . . From God and a woman. Man had nothing to do with him.

Sojourner Truth

It is really
asking too much
of a woman to
expect her to
bring up her
husband and her
children too.

Lillian Bell

An ounce
of mother is
worth a pound
of clergy.

Spanish proverb

Sometimes the strength of motherhood is greater than natural laws.

Barbara Kingsolver

A mother's love for her child is like nothing else in the world. It knows no law, no pity. It dares all things and crushes down remorselessly all that stands in its path.

Agatha Christie

I figure if the
kids are alive at
the end of the day,
I've done my job.

Roseanne Barr

53

chapter 6

Life

Seize the moment.
Remember all
those women on
the Titanic who
waved off
the dessert cart.

Erma Bombeck

You will do
foolish things, but do
them with enthusiasm.

Colette

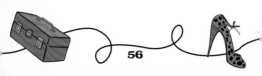

If you know you are going to fail, then fail gloriously.

Cate Blanchett

Another world is not only possible, she is on her way. On a quiet day, I can hear her breathing.

Arundhati Roy

As one goes
through life one
learns that if you
don't paddle your own
canoe, you don't move.

Katharine Hepburn

It's good to do uncomfortable things. It's weight training for life.

Anne Lamott

One must think like a hero to behave like a merely decent human being.

May Sarton

Grab the broom
of anger and
drive off the
beast of fear.

Zora Neale Hurston

This above all, to refuse to be a victim.

Margaret Atwood

Everything in moderation, including moderation.

Julia Child

Too much of a good thing can be wonderful.

Mae West

The vote means
nothing to women.
We should
be armed.

Edna O'Brien

I'll not listen to reason.
Reason always means what
someone else has got to say.

Elizabeth Cleghorn Gaskell

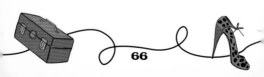

If only we'd stop
trying to be happy,
we could have a
pretty good time.

Edith Wharton

The contents of a handbag, like good whisky in a charred oak barrel, ripen and improve with age.

Peg Bracken

As time passes we all get better at blazing a trail through the thicket of advice.

Margot Bennett

Time and trouble will tame an advanced young woman, but an advanced old woman is uncontrollable by any earthly force.

Dorothy L. Sayers

**Gentle ladies,
you will
remember till
old age what
we did together
in our
brilliant youth!**

Sappho

**Freud is
the father of
psychoanalysis.
It has no mother.**

Germaine Greer

If you obey all the rules
you miss all the fun.

Katharine Hepburn

Considering how dangerous everything is, nothing is really very frightening.

Gertrude Stein

Adventure
is worthwhile
in itself.

Amelia Earhart

To live is so
startling it leaves little
time for anything else.

Emily Dickinson

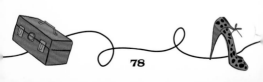

You only live
once, but if you
do it right, once
is enough.

Mae West

Women will have the last word.

Clara Schumann